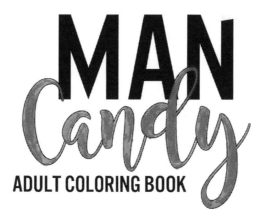

MAN Candy
ADULT COLORING BOOK

BY
USA TODAY BESTSELLING AUTHOR
VANESSA VALE

This book contains adult content and is not intended for children.

The author would like to credit the following for inspiration:
Period Images; Fotolia: Fxquadro, YakobchukOlena, ysbrandcosijn, Eugenio Marongiu, lordn, blackday, Tomasz Zajda, Sergey Nivens,
WavebreakmediaMicro; BigStock:fotorince, 1971yes, prometeus; Hot Damn Stock; Jenn LeBlanc/Illustrated Romance
Cover graphics: Hot Damn Stock & Bigstock: Andrey Armyagov

What's your favorite color? Mine too! We must be soulmates.

COLOR TEST PAGE.

I'D LOVE TO TOUCHDOWN IN YOUR END ZONE.

I COULD PUT SOME MOTION IN YOUR OCEAN.

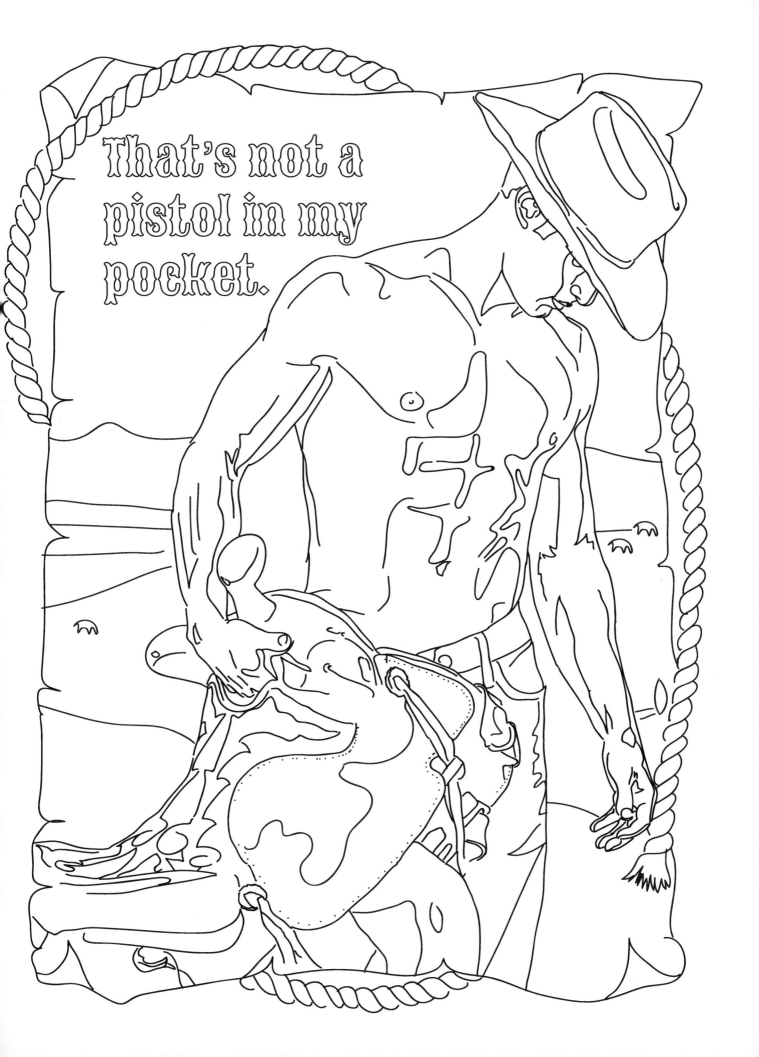

WHAT'S YOUR FAVORITE POSITION?

IS YOUR BATTERY DEAD?
'CAUSE I'D LOVE TO JUMP YOU.

IS THERE A MIRROR IN YOUR PANTS CAUSE I CAN SEE MYSELF IN THEM.

IF YOU WERE MY BIKE, I'D RIDE YOU EVERYDAY.

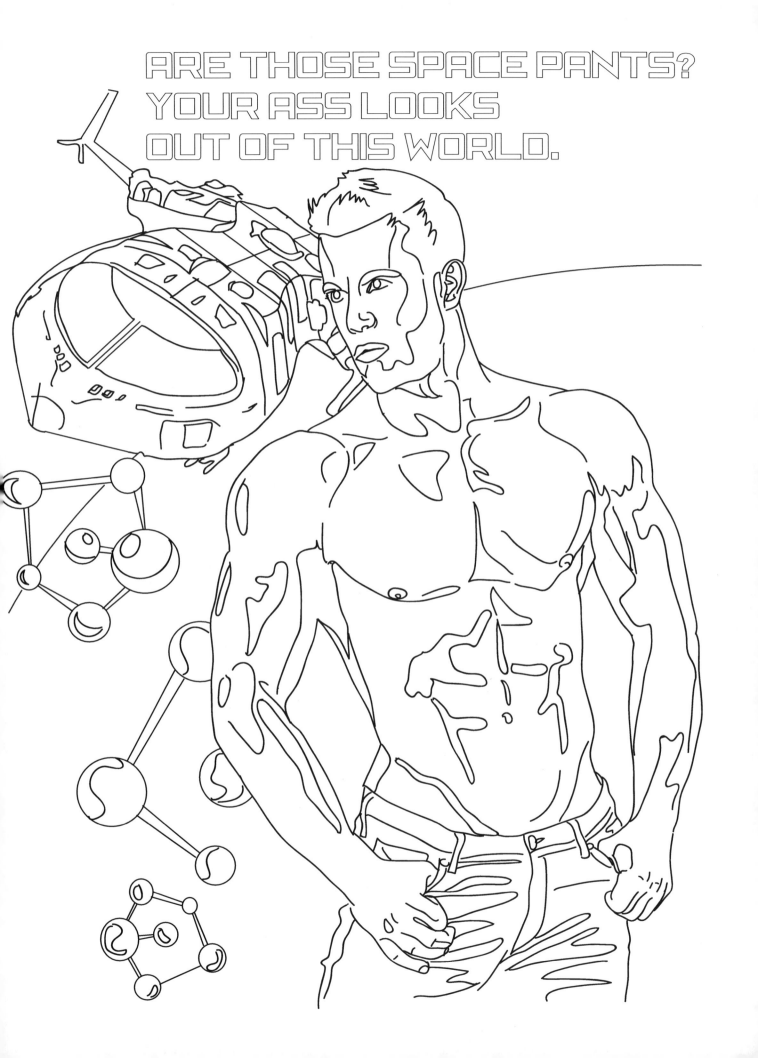

DO YOU HAVE SUNBURN OR ARE YOU ALWAYS THIS HOT?

WAS THAT AN EARTHQUAKE
OR DID I JUST ROCK YOUR WORLD?

Get 2 more Man Candy coloring pages FREE!

Go to: www.ksapublishing.com/coloring-pages

About the author:

Vanessa Vale is a *USA Today* Bestselling author of over twenty-five steamy erotic westerns. When she's not writing, Vanessa savors the insanity of raising two boys, is figuring out how many meals she can make with a pressure cooker, and teaches a pretty mean karate class. She considers herself to be remarkably normal, exceedingly introverted and fairly vanilla, which does not explain her steamy stories and her fascination with cowboys, preferably more than one at a time.

She lives in the Wild Wild West where there's an endless source of 'research' material.

www.vanessavaleauthor.com

www.ksapublishers.com

Made in the USA
Las Vegas, NV
15 February 2022